LIFE, STYLE, LEGACY

First published in 2026 by Welbeck
An imprint of HEADLINE PUBLISHING GROUP LIMITED

1

Cataloguing in Publication Data is available from the British Library

ISBN 978 1 03544 897 5

Printed and bound in China

MIX
Paper | Supporting responsible forestry
FSC® C008047
FSC
www.fsc.org

Headline's policy is to use papers that are neutral, renewable and recyclable products and made from wood grown in well-managed forests and other controlled sources. The logging and manufacturing processes are expected to conform to the environmental regulations of the country of origin.

HEADLINE PUBLISHING GROUP LIMITED
An Hachette UK Company
Carmelite House
50 Victoria Embankment
London EC4Y 0DZ

The authorised representative in the EEA is Hachette Ireland,
8 Castlecourt Centre, Dublin 15, D15 XTP3, Ireland (email: info@hbgi.ie)

www.headline.co.uk
www.hachette.co.uk

LIFE, STYLE, LEGACY

CBK

CAROLYN BESSETTE-KENNEDY:
THE STORY OF A FASHION ICON

GLENYS JOHNSON

WELBECK

CONTE

NTS

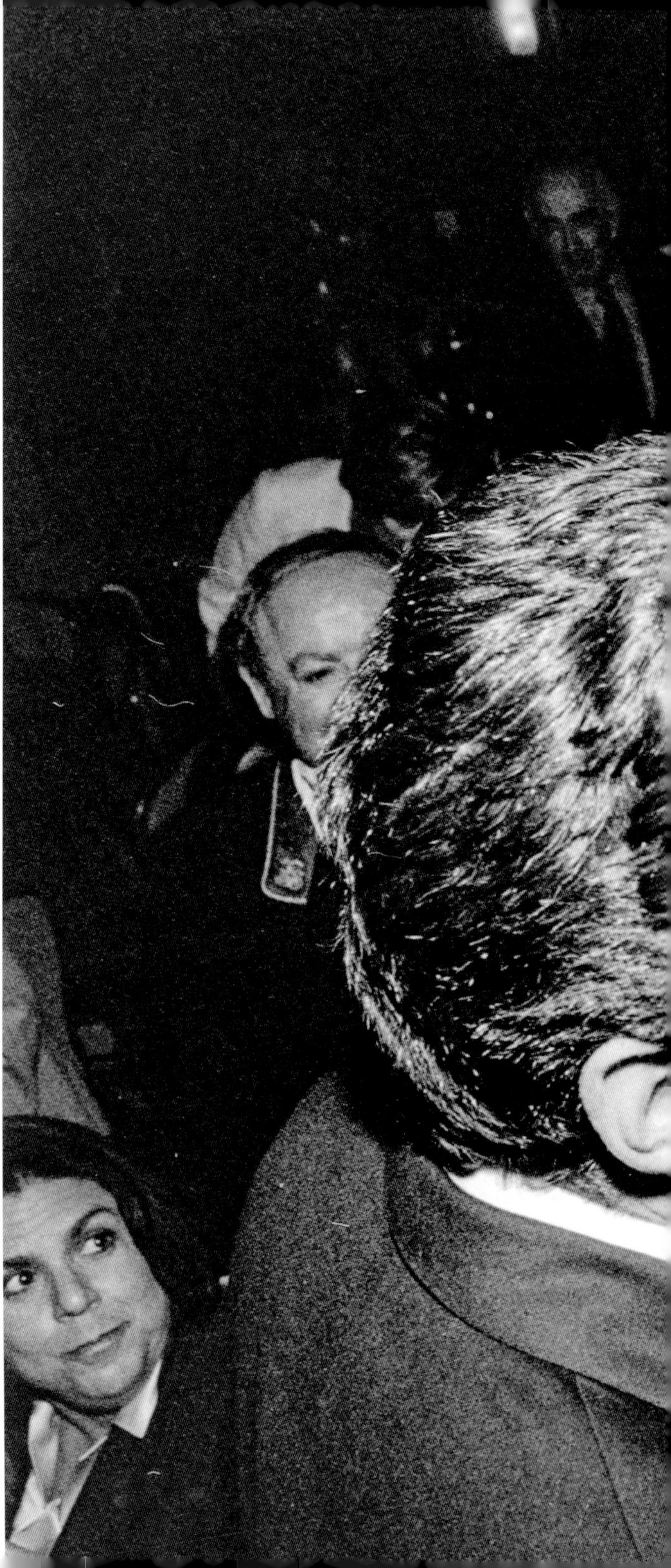

PREVIOUS PAGES Carolyn and JFK Jr. walk hand in hand, circa 1996

OPPOSITE Carolyn and husband JFK Jr. attend the Evelyn Lauder Breast Cancer Research Foundation luncheon, at the Waldorf Astoria in New York, 20 October 1998

INTRODUCTION

Examining the clothing worn by Carolyn Bessette-Kennedy over her relatively short stint in the spotlight is a somewhat complex task, perhaps ironic for a woman who is famous for her minimalistic approach to dressing. Carolyn was known to be a very private person, and most of the information available about her comes through second-hand accounts, including the information about her wardrobe. Thanks to dedicated fans (perhaps you, the reader, being one of them), many of Carolyn's looks have been dissected and garments identified, assigned to designers and specific collections. Some who knew Carolyn have shared stories about how she spoke of clothing or the shops she would visit around New York City. But many still find themselves with questions that will never be answered.

OPPOSITE Carolyn wore Yohji Yamamoto to attend *The Warhol Look: Glamour, Style, Fashion* exhibition gala with John, hosted by the Whitney Museum in November 1997

LINE DO N

For many of us, the clothing we choose to wear each day is a tool for self-expression. The same is true for those who live in the public eye – the difference, though, lies in the complexities of what they may like to express. Some of the most high-profile women in history have used clothing as a key tool for communication, Carolyn being one of the more recent to join the likes of Diana, Princess of Wales, and the woman who would have been her mother-in-law, Jackie Kennedy Onassis. Each of these women were thrust into the spotlight after marrying men of status, making them subjects of intrigue and inquisition across the world. Attempting to understand who Carolyn Bessette-Kennedy was as a person is simply not possible in the confines of this book, nor would a fashion writer be qualified to undertake such a task. But perhaps through summarizing what she wore alongside how and when she chose to wear it, we can observe the nuanced role of fashion not just in the world of a highly influential figure, but also as a cultural artefact to be analysed for its wider role in the world for generations to come.

OPPOSITE Carolyn, captured with her Comme des Garçons pouch, attending a film premiere in New York, circa January 1999

FASHIO

EVO

CHAPTER 1

N

LUTION

INTRODUCTION

"Some of it she had to be born with," *Allure*'s former editor-in-chief said, referring to Bessette-Kennedy's keen eye for style. "It was noticed by everyone who knew her in childhood and by the people who hired her in her early career in fashion."

Much of the analysis of Carolyn's style focuses on her years in the spotlight following her wedding to JFK Jr., which make up only a short period before their untimely deaths in 1999. It's important, however, to try to understand how the rest of her life played a role in creating the style icon that she became. As Carolyn was a notoriously private person and lived out her younger years long before social media became a part of our daily lives, dissecting these years and her relationship to fashion is no easy task. Here we'll attempt to understand some of the key influences that helped define Carolyn's taste and secure her as one of the most influential dressers of the 1990s.

OPPOSITE Carolyn Bessette wearing a leather jacket for the 1988 "Girls of Boston University" calendar

Carolyn

“Some of it she had to be born with.”

Allure's former editor-in-chief said, referring to Bessette-Kennedy's keen eye for style

OPPOSITE Carolyn Bessette's high school yearbook portrait from 1984

ABOVE Carolyn Bessette's childhood home
in Greenwich, Connecticut, pictured in 1997

THE EARLY YEARS

Carolyn Bessette was born on 7 January 1966 in White Plains, New York, a suburban area not far from New York City. Her mother was Ann Freeman, a teacher, and her father, William Joseph Bessette, a cabinetmaker. After her parents' divorce, Carolyn and her older twin sisters relocated to Connecticut with their mother, who then married Richard Freeman, an orthopaedic surgeon. The family's new home was situated in one of the more affluent neighbourhoods, providing a stable foundation for Carolyn's youth.

Even from Bessette's early days, people remarked on her knack for style, one classmate reportedly stating, "She was the only one who could pull off wearing ill-fitting school uniform pants." Another former peer told *The New York Times* in 1996, "She was in the beautiful 'in' crowd ... She went to all the right parties." Her classmates even reportedly voted her "Ultimate Beautiful Person" while at St Mary's High School.

From the images available, the teenage Bessette's sense of style wasn't unlike other girls of her age and what they were wearing across the United States. Light-wash denim jackets, chunky knits and polo tops were the norm. It's reported that Carolyn's grandmother, who she called "Nana", Jennie Messina, worked as a silkscreen artist for Vera Neumann – a renowned artist whose scarves were worn and adored by

OPPOSITE A 22-year-old Carolyn poses for a modelling job, wearing a leather jacket and cowboy boots

the likes of Grace Kelly and Marilyn Monroe. It's not known whether this influenced Carolyn and her developing style, but we can speculate that it may have exposed her to the industry beyond what she saw in the glossy magazines of the time.

By the mid 1980s, Bessette was working towards an undergraduate degree at Boston University, majoring in elementary education. According to her college roommate, Colleen Curtis, Bessette was a hard worker even in her younger years, working as a cocktail waitress to help fund her way through college. Bessette also dabbled in modelling, posing for the "Girls of BU" calendar and other smaller shoots. Some of the photographers who worked with her reported that she was a natural talent, but she ultimately decided that the vocation wasn't for her. "She couldn't sit still long enough. I think she's so smart, she wanted a better job," one cameraman told a magazine in a now resurfaced article.

After graduating in 1988, Bessette began working in retail at Calvin Klein in the Chestnut Hill Mall in Newton, Massachusetts, a western suburb of Boston. It was here that she would be able to lean into her love for clothes and use her natural charisma to charm customers and colleagues alike. This knack for managing demanding shoppers with noticeable ease, while looking like she had walked straight out of the pages of *Vogue*, was noticed by the area manager, who recommended her for a position at Calvin Klein's New York City HQ.

OPPOSITE The atrium of the Chestnut Hill Mall where Carolyn worked as a retail assistant before moving to New York, pictured here in 1985

“She was absolutely charming, she was completely refreshing, she was completely outgoing.”

Susan Sokol, a former Calvin Klein executive, said to have scouted Carolyn for her NYC role

OPPOSITE It’s reported that many compared Carolyn to the model Elaine Irwin, who modelled for Calvin Klein’s Fall/Winter 1989 campaign. Here Irwin can be seen on the runway for the Ralph Lauren Spring 1990 collection

"She couldn't sit still long enough. I think she's so smart, she wanted a better job."

A photographer who worked with young Carolyn

PREVIOUS PAGES Boston University, where Carolyn studied elementary education, pictured here in 1981

OPPOSITE Carolyn poses for portraits on 25 August 1992 in New York City

THE CALVIN KLEIN YEARS

As the eighties were coming to an end, Bessette was beginning her new life in New York City. Her first apartment in the city was said to be noticeably small inside ("even by New York standards," according to former flame Michael Bergin, as per his memoir). "I used to step over drunks and crack dealers to get into my apartment," Bessette remarked in a 1999 article with *Women's Wear Daily* (*WWD*). "Everybody at Calvin thought I was crazy. But I couldn't imagine coming to New York and living somewhere else. Even with all the weirdness, I felt comfortable and had fun."

As Bessette's life changed from fresh grad shopworker to twenty-something PR professional, the fashion landscape was changing too. The eighties were over and the style was moving away from the big hair and neon colours that had helped define it. "The key concepts in nineties fashion have been simplicity, neutrality and elegance. If anyone embodied that look, it was Carolyn," read an article honouring her in *Harpers & Queen* in September 1999.

OPPOSITE Carolyn wearing a dress from the 1992 Autumn/Winter collection, pictured with Calvin Klein himself at the City of Hope fundraiser party, New York, 28 October 1992

STEIN

"I'm not comfortable in anything ornate... I like clean, understated looks."

Carolyn told Glamour *in 1992*

PREVIOUS PAGES Carolyn backstage at the Calvin Klein Spring/Summer 1994 runway show, New York, 1993

LEFT A 27-year-old Carolyn and nightclub owner Will Regan at a Bloomingdale's event, New York, 3 March 1993

RESE
RITA

“Mr Klein, would often say, ‘I wonder how Carolyn would put this together.’ ”

A former Calvin Klein colleague told The New York Times *in 1996*

PREVIOUS PAGES Carolyn wore a silk top from the Calvin Klein Spring/Summer 1995 collection to Indochine's 10th anniversary, seen here with friends including Cari Regan and Kelly Klein, November 1994

OPPOSITE Kate Moss on the Calvin Klein runway for the Spring 1995 collection

ABSOLUTELY
NO
SMOKING

In *Champagne Supernovas*, a book that dissected the nineties, the American journalist Maureen Callahan highlighted Bessette's aesthetic at the time. "In mid-1992, this moment of grunge and grit and seventies regression, Bessette was nothing like the minimalist glamazon she became after marrying John F. Kennedy, Jr.: These days, she wore Egyptian musk and no make-up and had competitions with female Calvin staffers to see who could go the longest without washing her hair."

When Bessette arrived in NYC, Calvin Klein was going through a time of transition. The label had been struggling, with some stating it was on the verge of financial ruin. But with the help of Kate Moss, some risqué ads and the success of the label's fragrance line, Calvin Klein would quickly be on the up, becoming by the mid-nineties one of the world's most coveted brands, one that played a critical role in defining nineties style. Despite popular belief, Carolyn didn't discover Kate Moss, but she is said to have pushed for Calvin to select her to be the face of Calvin Klein's 1992 campaign, proving that her eye was a valuable asset to Mr Klein and his empire.

OPPOSITE Carolyn with Calvin Klein stylist Polly Hamilton backstage at a Calvin Klein fashion show, New York, 10 April 1994

In a *Harpers & Queen* feature on Bessette-Kennedy, Anne Marie Schiro, former fashion editor at *The New York Times*, commented on CBK's evolving style while at Calvin Klein: "At Calvin Klein, she shaped her look. She moved away from bouffant hair and denim jackets to the sleek, pared-down look that he favoured. Even if she wasn't always wearing Calvin Klein, she always epitomised his look."

As Carolyn climbed the ranks, her influence on the CK office style grew too. "Once she wore a long midi Calvin skirt with Chucks on her feet and only a fitted black leather jacket as a shirt," Elizabeth Beller, the author of *Once Upon a Time* (2025), shared. "Soon, Chucks, midi skirts and jackets as shirts made appearances all over the office."

OPPOSITE Carolyn working backstage at the Calvin Klein Fall/Winter 1995 runway show, held at the Gertrude Pavilion in Bryant Park, New York City, April 1995

“She has the look of the nineties. She is not a label girl – everything that she wore looked fabulous on her.”

Karl Lagerfeld,
WWD, *July 1999*

OPPOSITE A frequently referenced look, here we see Carolyn sporting a black turtleneck, cropped trousers and leather loafers as she stands with Calvin Klein colleague Jenny Landy, New York 1995

DKNY

Clare Waight Keller, the British fashion designer, began her career at Calvin Klein, and recalled Bessette-Kennedy's approach to dressing at the time in a piece for *Marie Claire*. "She'd come to the office looking as though she'd rolled out of bed. And then, when she had meetings, she'd transform herself from super-cool street-casual to the most elegant thing you'd ever seen." This dynamic is something that many who knew her remarked on over the years. Bessette's ability to balance a dedication to self-expression with somehow always being dressed appropriately is something that requires great skill and earned her a place on the Best Dressed lists over the years.

As she worked her way up the ranks at Calvin Klein, she began liaising with increasingly high-profile stars of the era. Some of her clients included the actors Annette Bening and Jennifer Aniston, and the journalist Diane Sawyer. Accounts vary on the details of exactly how Carolyn first crossed paths with her future husband, JFK Jr., though the reigning theory is that they were brought together through her role working with Calvin Klein's VIP clients. The rest, as they say, is history.

OPPOSITE Carolyn with Peter Berg at the 7th on Sale benefit for AIDS at the 26th Street Armory, New York City, 17 May 1995

RIGHT Carolyn, wearing a dress from the Fall/Winter 1995 Calvin Klein collection, poses with Jennifer Aniston in New York at the grand opening of 7th on Sale, a fundraiser for AIDS, 1995

THE KENNEDY YEARS

As her relationship with her future husband grew more serious, Carolyn's style also began to shift into something more mature and refined. One of the first images published in the press of Carolyn and JFK Jr. was of the pair sitting on the kerb observing the New York City marathon in November 1993. Carolyn wore a white tee, black jeans and a pair of chunky Derby shoes. Her hair is still a darker shade than it would later become, with strings of lighter strands scattered throughout. Other shots of Carolyn pre-wedding also showed a more relaxed style. In 1995 the couple were spotted at a NYC ATM with Carolyn in a knitted hat, oversized red sports jacket, black trousers and scuffed up trainers – a far cry from the sleek, understated approach for which she would become known.

> "Carolyn wasn't John's shadow; she was his equal."
>
> *RoseMarie Terenzio*

OPPOSITE For a function at the Hilton Hotel in New York on 1 June 1996 with JFK Jr., Carolyn wore a bateau neckline dress from Calvin Klein's 1995 Autumn/Winter collection

OPPOSITE Carolyn and John spotted on the streets of New York City, 20 September 1996

WALK
NYNEX

Elizabeth Beller, a friend of Carolyn's, relayed a key factor in Carolyn's approach to dressing as media interest in her increased. "She became obsessed with not giving the press anything to find wrong – a hair out of place, the wrong color or fit of clothes or having a scrap of dirt under her fingernails. There was a muting of herself – in her hair, body, style of dress – to make herself less remarkable, less accessible, less newsworthy ..." Some, including one former colleagues at Calvin Klein, speculated that her style evolved in line with her desire to be a "woman Jackie would have approved of" (referring to John's late mother, Jacqueline Kennedy Onassis). Whether this was the case, or perhaps it was simply a natural shift into a sleeker wardrobe, which is experienced by many women moving into their late twenties and early thirties, Bessette-Kennedy's minimalist wardrobe of logo-free staple pieces began to take shape. Just a few months after Carolyn and JFK Jr.'s secret wedding on Cumberland Island, some of the world's top fashion editors were recognizing her impeccable taste. Speaking to *Newsweek* in October 1996, *Vogue*'s Anna Wintour proclaimed, "Carolyn has fabulous modern style." *Harper's Bazaar*'s Liz Tilberis added, "She's going to be an amazing symbol of American style."

OPPOSITE Pictured here with husband John on 4 November 1996, Carolyn wore a black Prada dress and coat with Manolo Blahnik shoes to the 30th anniversary of the Whitney Museum in New York

One of the most notable shifts in Carolyn's style came in the form of her now-famous golden mane. For much of the 1990s, Carolyn's hair was what her former hairstylist, Brad Johns, referred to as a "toffee" shade. Her blonde hair could easily warrant an entire book of its own, but we'll get into it in more detail later. For now, we'll just touch on its role in Carolyn's style evolution into her role as a Kennedy. Brad Johns once commented on this transformation direction: "Since John Kennedy married her, she became more regal ... So now I make her hair a paler blond with a hint of Grace Kelly demureness, which is how she wants to present herself." And it seems this makeover worked wonders: in a 1999 piece following her death, *Harpers & Queen* dubbed her "The most elegant woman in America."

A big part of being married to John F. Kennedy Jr. was attending high-profile events. It quickly became clear that these were Carolyn's opportunity to present herself in a controlled environment – one where she was in the driver's seat and not being cornered by cameras while taking her beloved dog Friday out for a morning walk. Many have analysed Carolyn's love for Yohji Yamamoto, speculating that her affinity for wearing the Japanese designer's pieces to evening

OPPOSITE A rare sighting of Carolyn wearing jewellery, here in the form of a simple pearl necklace, styled with a Prada dress under a black coat, 11 October 1996

BARNEYS
NEW YORK

"The key concepts in nineties fashion have been simplicity, neutrality and elegance. If anyone embodied that look, it was Carolyn. Camel, beige and black suited her honey-coloured hair to perfection; her hair fell naturally into the required straight waterfall."

Harpers & Queen,
September 1999

PREVIOUS PAGES Carolyn and John at the Municipal Art Society of New York Benefit, 22 September 1996

OPPOSITE Carolyn wearing a Prada coat, boots and Spazzolato leather tote, walking along Varick Street in Manhattan with John, 23 October 1996

events went deeper than being attracted to his clean lines and playful structures, and reflected an embrace of his design philosophy. "I make clothing like armour," Yamamoto remarked in a 2011 interview. "I wanted to protect the clothes themselves from fashion, and at the same time protect the woman's body from something." This connection has been most thoroughly analysed by fashion critic Rachel Tashjian, who has referred to Bessette as Yamamoto's "great interpreter" in various pieces for *GQ* and *The Washington Post*.

Away from these red-carpet occasions, Carolyn's everyday outfits were often captured by paparazzi as she went about her daily life in New York City – running errands and catching up with friends. Her looks were practical and appropriate for the city's sometimes difficult climate. When the weather was warm, she wore plain T-shirts with a simple skirt. In the colder months, she threw on a wool coat, jeans and knee-high leather boots. Carolyn's hair was often worn down (no big volume blowouts here) or styled with one of her signature tortoiseshell headbands.

OPPOSITE When she was running daily errands in New York City, Carolyn's style was dressed down and casual, as seen here on 28 August 1997

Warbird
Flight
508 693-1485

"She never looks studied. I've seen her wear an inexpensive T-shirt and an expensive jacket. That shows personal expression. She doesn't tear a page out of a magazine and recreate the look."

Designer Michael Kors in a 1996 Newsweek *piece titled "Crazy for Carolyn"*

OPPOSITE Carolyn and John at the second anniversary party for *George* magazine, at the Asia de Cuba restaurant in New York on 5 November 1997

OPPOSITE Carolyn in a Yohji Yamamoto houndstooth suit at the opening of the Saks Fifth Avenue men's store in San Francisco on 19 September 1997

ABOVE Model walks the runway at the Yohji Yamamoto ready-to-wear Fall 1997 collection on 15 March 1997 in Paris

ABOVE Donatella Versace, Carolyn Bessette-Kennedy and John F. Kennedy Jr. attending "An Evening at La Fenice", a benefit held on 2 December 1997 at Carnegie Hall in New York

ABOVE Another outing with Carolyn wearing Yohji Yamamoto, this time from the label's Spring/Summer 1997 collection. Carolyn wore the design to honour the 80th anniversary of JFK's birth on 29 May 1997

In many ways, Carolyn's wardrobe wasn't too dissimilar to that of any woman in her late twenties working in fashion and living in the Upper East Side in the mid to late 1990s – but it was definitely different from what one would expect from the wardrobe of a wife to a Kennedy. By most accounts, Carolyn had the fashion world at her fingertips. If she had wanted to wear a new designer dress every day and have her hair and make-up done immaculately, sitting front row at every show at New York fashion week, she would have been welcomed with open arms. But that wasn't her style. Carolyn preferred a streamlined approach

"She is the walking creation. She is the woman of taste and dignity."

Yohji Yamamoto

OPPOSITE Carolyn wore a cape design rumoured to be from Yohji Yamamoto as she and John attended the Jacqueline Kennedy Onassis Medal ceremony at the Municipal Art Society, New York City, 1997

OPPOSITE A model walks the runway at the Yohji Yamamoto Spring 1998 ready-to-wear runway show on 18 October 1997 in Paris

ABOVE Carolyn in the Yohji jacket pictured opposite, with JFK Jr., on their way to the Profile in Courage Awards in Boston, 29 May 1998

– she liked what she liked, and she didn't feel the need to complicate things. In 2005, Carole Radziwill, friend of Carolyn and wife of JFK Jr.'s cousin, Anthony Radziwill, released a memoir that explained how Carolyn's dress sense was also shaped by the press attention. "We came up with the idea ... that she'd wear the same outfit every day – jeans and a white shirt, with her hair in a ponytail and sunglasses – and then the pictures would all look the same. And they'd stop taking them." Curiously, this strategy may have been one of the key reasons she became such a style icon.

"She let her clothes do most of the talking."

Rachel Tashjian for The Washington Post

OPPOSITE A smiling Carolyn sports opera-length gloves and red lipstick for a White House visit with John, February 1998

ABOVE Carolyn at the Supper Club at an after party following a performance by the Parsons Dance Company, May 1998

ABOVE A model wears the same outfit worn by Carolyn (opposite) on the Paris runway for the Yohji Yamamoto Spring 1998 ready-to-wear presentation, on 18 October 1997

“Carolyn has fabulous modern style.”

Anna Wintour for Newsweek, 1996

OPPOSITE Carolyn wore a poncho and dress set from Yohji Yamamoto's Autumn/Winter 1998 collection to the Breast Cancer Research Foundation benefit in New York on 20 October 1998

ABOVE Carolyn wearing Yohji Yamamoto Spring/ Summer 1998 ready-to-wear, with John at a fundraising dinner benefit for Riverkeeper World Trade Center in New York on 2 April 1998

ABOVE Big smiles from Carolyn, in a Yohji Yamamoto ruffled coat, at the May 1999 "Newman's Own" *George* Awards

ABOVE Carolyn enjoying Thanksgiving
weekend at Hyannis, Cape Cod, 1997

KEY

CHAPTER 2

LOOKS

INTRODUCTION

Throughout her short reign as what many have referred to as "America's answer to Princess Diana", Carolyn donned a handful of looks that sit apart from the rest. In this chapter we'll examine some of the outfits that continue to be referenced again and again by designers and everyday fans alike, even decades after her passing. From black-tie events where she mixed with some of the world's top leaders of the decade to a quick stroll around Tribeca with her husband, Carolyn had a sense of style that shone through, resonating with and inspiring women across the globe.

FORMAL AFFAIRS

Though Carolyn was spotted on the arm of JFK Jr. at some official events before their 1996 wedding, her approach to dressing for those occasions was less formal than it became after their nuptials. For a Cartier reception at the Château de Maligny in Switzerland a few months before their wedding, Carolyn wore a dress from Calvin Klein's Spring/Summer 1996 collection, featuring a jersey construction and sleeveless cut – a simple and chic look, but not quite the structured tailoring pieces that she would go on to make her signature. Following the wedding, Carolyn's formal styles would become an opportunity to communicate with the world while championing the talents of her designer friends and labels she admired. Here we'll explore some of her most iconic looks.

OPPOSITE Carolyn and JFK Jr. at an official White House dinner hosted by US President Bill Clinton, in honour of Great Britain's Prime Minister Tony Blair, February 1998

THE WEDDING DRESS

Though the press had shown interest in Carolyn's style since she first began dating JFK Jr., the event that quickly thrust her into fashion magazines across the globe was none other than her own wedding. The pair married in a private ceremony in a small chapel on Cumberland Island in Georgia on the evening of 21 September 1996. Carolyn requested that her close friend and Calvin Klein colleague Narciso Rodriguez design the dress, a responsibility he was keen to accept. "I made that wedding dress with so much love for the person that I loved most in the whole world," Rodriguez told PBS in 2020.

At the time, frilly princess-style gowns were still very much the accepted style for brides, but Carolyn and Narciso were ready to go against the grain. Carolyn's dress was crafted from ivory silk tulle in a slip dress design with a cowl neck style. Her shoes were said to be sandals courtesy of Manolo Blahnik, and she wore sheer opera-style gloves, displayed in the famous photo of the couple walking down the church steps. There were no ornate floral arrangements, instead a simple bunch of lily-of-the-valley flowers. As a nod to her husband's late mother, Carolyn reportedly wore a hair clip that had belonged to Jacqueline Kennedy Onassis to secure her low bun.

PREVIOUS PAGES Donning a sleeveless jersey maxi dress from the Calvin Klein Spring/Summer 1996 collection, Carolyn accompanied John to Zurich, Switzerland, for a Cartier reception at Château de Maligny in April 1996

OPPOSITE *LIFE* magazine cover featuring Carolyn's iconic wedding dress from her September 1996 wedding to JFK Jr

THE YEAR IN PICTURES
LIFE
LOVE BLOOMS (SOMETIMES)
Kennedys. AH-H-H!
Royals: OOPS!
Michael Jackson: HUH?
WEATHER REIGNS
Hurricanes! Fires! Blizzards! Floods!
AMERICA MOURNS
The victims of TWA 800 and ValuJet 592
WOMEN SOAR, KIDS RULE
First Wives, Soccer Moms, Kerri, Shannon, Rosie, Liv
MARS ROCKS
Aliens invade.
...AND FRIENDS DEPART
George Burns, Gene Kelly, Ella Fitzgerald, Erma Bombeck, Tupac Shakur
1996
WHAT A YEAR!
JANUARY 1997/$4.95
COLLECTOR'S EDITION

"The idea of the slip dress as wedding dress for that time was revolutionary... Its simplicity was shocking."

Kate Betts, former editor in chief of Harper's Bazaar

OPPOSITE The wedding dress that changed it all. Carolyn and John leaving the First African Baptist Church on Cumberland Island, Georgia, 21 September 1996

The dress inspired plenty of lookalikes to pop up in shops across America and abroad, a trend that has continued for decades following the nuptials. In a *New York Times* article from January 1997, journalist Constance C.R. White noted that "the simple bridal gown has crystallized an emerging trend: the idea of an alternative bride who eschews froufrou in favor of stylish understatement." And, in this instance, it seems that White was very much right. Writing in 2021, American fashion journalist Kate Betts shared her view that the dress "was revolutionary in that sense, that someone would wear something that simple." She continued, "It crystallized that trend [minimalism] in fashion. That was her aesthetic, and her wedding dress was a very, very bold expression of that minimalism."

ABOVE Narciso Rodriguez, the close friend of Carolyn and designer of her iconic wedding dress and rehearsal dress, defined by its embellished crystals and slip dress silhouette. Rodriguez poses here with a model, September 1996

ABOVE One of the many lookalike dresses to appear in storefronts after the September 1996 wedding. This one complete with cardboard cut-out of John

20-26 N.MOORE ST
LOFTS FOR

THE DOUBLE-BREASTED SKIRT SUIT

One of the first formal events attended by the couple after their wedding the previous autumn was a Municipal Art Society gala on 4 March 1997, where actor Robert De Niro was awarded the Jacqueline Kennedy Onassis Medal. CBK wore a structured jacket by Yohji Yamamoto alongside a skirt from Comme des Garçons. The jacket would be one of the first of similar styles worn to black-tie occasions, showcasing her love for avant-garde Japanese design and her sleek and minimalist style. Carolyn is reported to have gifted the pieces to RoseMarie Terenzio, John F. Kennedy Jr.'s Executive Assistant at *George* magazine and a friend of the couple. The outfit appeared at Sotheby's "Fashion Icons" auction in 2024. In a statement accompanying the auction, Lucy Bishop, fashion specialist at Sotheby's, remarked: "These garments speak volumes about her tragically short but remarkable life ... They reveal a woman who made considered choices, navigated public scrutiny with intelligence and grace, displaying a generosity and kindness that touched those around her. Carolyn Bessette-Kennedy understood the power of dressing well, and this belief is forever reflected in these clothes."

OPPOSITE Carolyn, wearing Yohji Yamamoto Spring 1997 skirt suit and Manolo Blahnik shoes, heads to the Municipal Art Society in New York with John on 4 March 1997

"For me, timeless design is when you combine the past, the present and the future, and she's an extreme example."

Designer Gabriela Hearst for Vanity Fair

OPPOSITE Carolyn's 1997 Yohji Yamamoto jacket and Comme des Garçons skirt on display for auction at Sotheby's "Fashion Icons" sale in 2024

CLOSED
Use alternate entrances.

THE STRAPLESS STYLE

When it comes to her formalwear looks, many associate Bessette-Kennedy with the pairing of a strapless black dress and opera gloves. The reality is, however, that CBK only wore strapless designs a handful of times, one of them being on an October evening in 1998 to the Municipal Art Society's revitalization of Grand Central Terminal. There are many reasons why this look has imprinted itself on the brains of many; perhaps it's simply one that is circulated by media outlets more often than others, or perhaps it has a special way of bringing out Bessette's innate style. Whatever the reason, this ensemble is definitely one of her most iconic. The dress is credited to Yohji Yamamoto's Autumn/Winter 1998 collection and was worn with velvet opera gloves and Manolo Blahnik heels. Bessette also wore a single gold bracelet on her right wrist, one that had reportedly belonged to Jackie Kennedy Onassis. JFK Jr. also appeared to be a fan of this look, telling reporters on the red carpet: "You gotta see the back. The back's the best part!"

OPPOSITE Carolyn at the Grand Central Terminal revitalization event in New York City, 5 October 1998

THE WHITE SKIRT LOOK

On 1 June 1998, Carolyn attended a benefit for the Robin Hood Foundation with JFK Jr., who sat on the board of the NYC charity. Her outfit came courtesy of the Spring/Summer 1998 collection by Yohji Yamamoto. The jacket featured a collarless design with raw edging, a corset-style structure and 19 front buttons. Carolyn opted to pair it with a white skirt that sat just below the knee, and a pair of leather Manolo Blahnik heels. The jacket and skirt look was also featured in a *Vogue Italia* spread in January 1998 alongside Naomi Campbell wearing a dress from the same Yohji Yamamoto 1998 Spring/Summer collection. The same style was worn by Carolyn in August 1998 when she and John attended a wedding in Italy. Carolyn wore this button-clad number to the Riverkeeper dinner benefit at the World Trade Center a few months earlier. For that outing, it was worn with a matching black silk skirt. Winona Ryder, another nineties style icon, wore the same Yohji Yamamoto look on the red carpet of the premiere for Season 5 of *Stranger Things* in November 2025, proving the lasting influence of CBK.

OPPOSITE Carolyn wore a striking Yohji Yamamoto jacket and white skirt to a benefit for the Robin Hood Foundation with John on 1 June 1998

OPPOSITE A model walks in the Yohji Yamamoto Spring 1998 ready-to-wear show on 18 October 1997, in Paris. She wears the same black, buttoned jacket worn by CBK at the June 1998 Robin Hood Foundation benefit

ABOVE A model walks the runway at the Yohji Yamamoto Fall 1998 ready-to-wear show on 15 March 1998, in Paris

THE VERSACE COAT DRESS

Trading in her usual all-black approach for evening events, Carolyn made headlines in December 1998 by stepping out to the Fire & Ice Ball in LA wearing a white floor-length dress by Versace. The basket-weave coat dress was from the first Versace collection constructed following Gianni Versace's death in July 1997 and was crafted using an 8-ply cashmere/wool/silk blend and front zip fastening. "It's timeless but modern in the same time," designer Gabriela Hearst told *Vanity Fair* in 2017, recalling the outfit. "For me, timeless design is when you combine the past, the present and the future, and she's an extreme example." Jørgen Simonsen, former head designer at Versace, took to his social media in February 2026 to recall Carolyn in the design, speculating that the dress appealed to Carolyn due to its minimalist design – a departure from the fashion house's usual maximalist approach. Carolyn was friends with both Gianni and Donatella Versace, often being invited to spend time with the designer duo at their home in Lake Como, Italy. She was one of the many high-profile guests at Gianni's funeral at Milan Cathedral, seated just a few rows behind Princess Diana.

OPPOSITE Carolyn smiling in Versace at the Ninth Annual Fire & Ice Ball in Los Angeles, 9 December 1998

THE WHITE SHIRT STYLE

Instantly recognizable as a CBK classic, the white shirt and black skirt look is one of the most reproduced outfits Carolyn provided us in her short time in the fashion spotlight. Carolyn wore this look to a gala at the Whitney Museum in March 1999. The white button-down shirt with the sleeves rolled up, and the floor-length black skirt with ruffles across the lower half, were from Yohji Yamamoto's Spring/Summer 1999 collection. Carolyn, however, never one to carbon copy anything, went against the runway's styling and paired the pieces herself, playing with an off-kilter buttoning of the top and tucking it into the skirt's waistband. The accessories of the night consisted of a small gold-tone bag courtesy of Whiting & Davis and her trusted patent leather Manolo Blahnik Callasli sandals. The look has since prompted plenty of reviews from fashion publications around the world, many listing it as one of her most memorable. Aside from its aesthetic appeal, the ensemble also perfectly exemplifies why Yamamoto's designs may have appealed to Carolyn, something Anne-Marie Schiro articulated in a 1999 article in *Harpers & Queen*: "they don't look like anybody else's. They have a little twist to them that is elegant but not as simplistic as Calvin Klein. Yohji's cut gives an edge to a very simple line, and I think that Carolyn liked that because it gave her a very distinctive look that was never outrageous."

OPPOSITE Carolyn and John F. Kennedy Jr. returning home after an evening at the Whitney Museum in March 1999

THE WHITE HOUSE DINNER OUTFIT

On 1 May 1999, Carolyn and John attended the annual White House Correspondents' Dinner, joined by actor Sean Penn. Carolyn's outfit for the evening remains one of her most memorable: in a *Vogue* article from September 1999, the late Charles Gandee said that it stood as one of the two he most remembered (the other being the strapless Yohji Yamamoto gown worn in October 1998). In 2026, the look was again referenced as a fan favourite by Rosa Sanchez of *Harper's Bazaar*, who hoped that it would be recreated in *Love Story*, the television series by Ryan Murphy which was released in February that year. "It was sleek and minimalist, but bold at the same time, which is exactly what I love about her style," Sanchez remarked.

Carolyn opted for a Jean Paul Gaultier look for the occasion, straying from her usual dedication to Yohji Yamamoto. The double-breasted jacket featured peaked lapels, which she wore with her signature slicked-back bun and a red lip. While it looks as though Carolyn is wearing a fan-shape necklace under the jacket, the Jean Paul Gaultier 1999 collection featured an identical fan feature that attached to a transparent tulle bodice. However, Carolyn wore the jacket buttoned throughout the evening, so it's unclear whether the design matched the one from the runway. The image of Carolyn and JFK Jr. cuddling at the event was often used to depict their relationship following their death a few months later, securing its spot as one of the most recognized images of the pair.

ABOVE Carolyn, wearing a Jean Paul Gaultier look, and John cuddle at the annual White House Correspondents' Dinner in Washington, D.C. on 1 May 1999

THE JFK FOUNDATION DINNER

The 1999 JFK Foundation Dinner held in Boston on 23 May was the final official public event attended by the couple. In many ways, the outfit worn that evening by Bessette-Kennedy was the perfect look in which to leave the public eye – it was by her favourite designer, Yohji Yamamoto, and embodied everything Carolyn represented throughout her reign as one of the world's best-dressed women. The tailored design was a part of the Japanese label's Autumn/Winter 1998 collection, complete with sharp shoulders, notched lapel and cinched waist. Carolyn's hair was slicked back into a neat bun and bright red lipstick was the only colour she wore. She marked the occasion with a set of simple pearl stud earrings, a departure from her usual no-jewellery approach. Though Carolyn and Yohji Yamamoto never had the chance to meet, Carolyn is said to have had a relationship with the brand since she started sporting its designs in 1996. "It was very natural for Carolyn to come in, she was like a fixture in our store. She came in about every two months or so," one former shopworker recalled in 2025. Yohji Yamamoto himself also publicly spoke about his love for Carolyn, most famously in 1999, when he told *WWD*: "She is the walking creation. She is the woman of taste and dignity."

OPPOSITE Carolyn and John at the JFK Library Foundation dinner in Boston on 23 May 1999

OFF-DUTY STYLE

Though the looks CBK wore to evening events demonstrated her talent for styling sleek ensembles that showcased her love for particular fashion houses, it was her everyday outfits that have truly cemented her as a style icon all these years later. Season after season we see brands pay homage to her off-duty style with lookbook imagery mimicking grainy paparazzi images of lookalikes on New York City streets. It's Carolyn's casual jeans and tee looks that women across the world analysed in the glossy magazines at the time and which continue to be dissected across social media accounts today. These looks give us the best idea of what Carolyn loved and valued in her wardrobe when the dress code wasn't black tie.

OPPOSITE Carolyn wearing her off-duty staples including Selima Optique sunglasses and Charles Wahba headband, in New York City on 10 October 1996

THE NEWLYWEDS LOOK

One of CBK's most instantly recognizable looks (and undeniably the one most recreated by fans of her sartorial choices) has to be the outfit from 6 October 1996. John F. Kennedy Jr. and Carolyn Bessette had tied the knot in their secret ceremony a few months earlier, and by all accounts, Carolyn was surprised and somewhat startled by the press attention that had been forming outside the couple's front door. The pair decided to pose for the paparazzi in the hopes that this would satiate the press and reduce the feeding frenzy, something that Carolyn is said to have been extra aware of following the death of Princess Diana a few months earlier.

The outfit that Carolyn decided to wear was one which really defined her everyday look. A cashmere Prada sweater was paired with a camel skirt from Prada's Autumn/Winter 1996 collection. The skirt's hem sat just below the knee, a cut that some say she helped to popularize at the time. The leather boots were also credited to Prada, defined by their knee-high cut, rich cognac colour and slim, decorative ankle strap. The look was finished by one of Carolyn's favourite bags at the time, the Prada Spazzolato bag, a patent leather tote design.

OPPOSITE Carolyn wears head-to-toe Prada as her new husband introduces her to the press outside their home in New York on 6 October 1996

“Prada was her ultimate north star.”

Renee Washington for Grazia

OPPOSITE Model Trish Goff on the runway for the Prada Fall 1996 collection in Milan on 7 March 1996

THE JEANS AND BUN LOOK

A favourite among the countless fan accounts across social media dedicated to Carolyn's style, the jeans and bun look encompasses many of the elements that defined Carolyn's fashion. Featuring a slicked-back bun with headband, a roll-neck jumper, wool coat, jeans and loafers – this look packs a lot in. This image is from an afternoon in mid-October 1997, reportedly captured just after the couple had lunch at one of their go-to spots in their neighbourhood, Bubby's. In February 2026, *Cosmopolitan*'s Kelsey Stiegman said that this look could "singlehandedly be credited for the return of flare jeans." The jacket is thought to be one of her trusted Prada styles, worn with a black turtleneck, Levi 517s and leather loafers by Manolo Blahnik. This is one of the looks recreated in the TV series *Love Story* (2026).

OPPOSITE Carolyn, in one of her most referenced looks, after brunch with John on 18 October 1997

THE TURTLENECK AND CORDS LOOK

In May 1999, Carolyn and John were spotted in Manhattan, with Carolyn sporting a look consisting of a black turtleneck jumper, a pair of loafers, her Hermès Birkin 40 and signature sunglasses. This look has been dissected by many of the social media accounts dedicated to Carolyn's style – some praising it for its mixed textures (corduroy, knitwear and leather) and sleek proportions that complement Carolyn's statuesque physique. This look is a testament to the style philosophy that Carolyn shared in a 1992 *Glamour* interview, an ethos she retained long after becoming an A-lister, "If I want to add some impact, I'll do it with texture."

OPPOSITE Carolyn and John take a springtime stroll through New York, May 1999

Carolyn's love affair with this pair of corduroy trousers seems to have begun around October 1997, when the style star was first spotted wearing the toffee-coloured bottoms while out in New York. On that occasion, she was seen wearing them with a leather blazer and black top with a copy of the October 1997 issue of *W* magazine under her arm. A few weeks later, she wore them again while shopping in Tribeca with a Prada puffer jacket and leather loafers. The lore behind the trousers is that Carolyn picked them up at Cheap Jack's, a second-hand shop in downtown Manhattan. The brand, however, is much contested, though *Vogue* identifies it as Helmut Lang.

OPPOSITE Carolyn, John and their dog Friday enjoy an autumn day in New York, October 1997

ABOVE In 1996, Carolyn steps
out with John wearing a pair of
nineties classics, Nike Air Streaks

ABOVE Carolyn wearing tan chinos, a dark top and an Hermès belt on honeymoon with husband JFK Jr. in Istanbul, Turkey, 1996

THE SAILING LOOK

For Thanksgiving 1997, Carolyn and JFK Jr. took a trip to the Kennedy Compound in Hyannisport, Massachusetts. It was during this trip that the couple were photographed heading off to meet Ted Kennedy for a day of sailing, with Carolyn sporting a leisurewear look that would go on to become one of the more frequently referenced outfits for CBK admirers. The jacket is said to be a Brown's Beach Jacket, a style that dates back to the early years of the twentieth century. The technique used to create the "beach cloth" is said to have been created by fusing wool and cotton fabrics to create something tough enough to keep workers warm through the Massachusetts winters. The design continues to be a coveted style for fans of highly functional heritage pieces. The bag worn here also sprouts from a utilitarian American workwear foundation, standing the test of time since its realization in 1944. The LL Bean Boat and Tote bag was originally created as a tool to transport blocks of ice, but was quickly discontinued before re-appearing (and taking on the nautical title) in the sixties and being positioned as a tool for lugging around goods for boating trips. The charm of this look definitely lies in its dedication to classic WASP style, pairing two staples of the style in one look. And with a Kennedy on your arm, it doesn't get more American than that.

OPPOSITE Carolyn goes for an all-American look during a sailing trip in Hyannisport on Thanksgiving weekend, 1997

STYLE

S

CHAPTER 3

TAPLES

INTRODUCTION

Journalist Bethan Holt once said, "CBK had the power to transform an item with her personal brand of relaxed sophistication." And the fact that the woman with one of the most understated wardrobes has also become one of the most admired style icons of the twentieth century certainly proves this power. Carolyn's relatively small collection of clothes was often mixed and matched with ease due to their versatility and colour palette of mostly black, white, tan and navy. Here we'll explore some of her most prized styles, how she wore them and what their significance may be.

OPPOSITE Carolyn at the Annual Fundraising Gala at the Whitney Museum of American Art in New York City on 9 March 1999

ABOVE Carolyn wearing Oakley sunglasses, a navy shirt, straight leg trousers and leather Prada loafers on Madison Avenue in New York City, 15 July 1997

THE BUTTON-DOWN SHIRTS

Showing just how impactful that Yohji Yamamoto look was from her night at the Whitney in March 1999, a button-down shirt has easily become one of the key pieces for which Carolyn is remembered. CBK was also spotted wearing the staple style on a trip to Hyannis for the Kennedys' Labor Day weekend gathering in 1997. On a warm July day in 1997, Carolyn was also captured wearing a slightly more fitted button-down shirt in a darker, navy colour as she strolled down Madison Avenue. The former PR exec wore the shirt with its sleeves rolled up past the elbow and the first few buttons undone, resulting in a relaxed approach that helped define her look. But Carolyn's love for shirts goes back from before she became America's princess. In 1992, while working at Calvin Klein, Carolyn appeared in the pages of *Glamour* opposite model Lauren Hutton, sporting a men's Calvin Klein shirt with the sleeves rolled up to the shoulders, styled with a pair of dark jeans.

Though we know that the shirt worn to the Whitney was a Yohji Yamamoto design, there's not much information available about the exact styles she wore on other occasions. Perhaps, the white button-down top has become so heavily associated with her because of its undeniable versatility, rather than due to the beauty of the particular garment. The 1992 piece in *Glamour* was meant to show the shirt's ability to work with the wardrobes of a wide array of women – from a humble CK publicist to a supermodel like Hutton. If only the people behind the shoot had understood just how the young unknown would play a key role in reimagining the shirt in women's wardrobes across the world just a few years later.

"She chose the simplest pieces from the conceptual greats – that is itself a talent, and befitting of her low-key elegance."

Emma Elwick for Harper's Bazaar

OPPOSITE Carolyn enjoys Labor Day weekend in Hyannisport, 1997

THE FOOTWEAR

Carolyn's footwear styles have been another key area of interest for fans over the years. For formal occasions, she was known to cycle through a few favourite styles, including the Manolo Blahnik Callasli heels and another Manolo pair by the name of Carolyne. The latter was defined by a pointed toe and slingback style and, despite what some may assume, wasn't named after Carolyn but was in fact inspired by Carolyne Roehm, a muse of the renowned shoemaker. The Callasli style offered a criss-cross strap feature and a slingback heel, an addition to the original design, said to have been encouraged by Anna Wintour.

For more casual outfits, Carolyn seems to have adored a pair of Prada sandals with the name Capretto, another strappy design but this time with a block heel and in a neutral colourway that the label called "tabacco". Carolyn was captured wearing the summer style with jeans, while on honeymoon with JFK Jr. in Turkey, and taking Friday out for a walk. The pair are fan favourites, and plenty of forum threads are dedicated to people trying to hunt down their own pair. Another casual option that Carolyn reached for on summer days was a simple pair of flip-flops, which she often styled with jeans and a casual top. Havaianas were reportedly her go-to.

OPPOSITE A warm autumn day out with Friday, Carolyn wears one of her favourite pairs of jeans, a sleeveless black top and her Prada Capretto sandals, 5 October 1996

“Carolyn Bessette-Kennedy embodied the essence of New York style: effortless and utterly timeless. The way she dressed then feels just as modern today, which is the true mark of elegance.”

Manolo Blahnik, Footwear News

OPPOSITE Carolyn with Lee Radziwill, sister of Jacqueline Kennedy Onassis, at the Grand Central Terminal reopening reception in New York City on 6 September 1998

Leather loafers are probably the shoe most associated with Carolyn, featuring in a number of her most popular off-duty outfits. Her closet held Prada loafers in an array of styles, from polka-dot pony skin from the label's Autumn/Winter 1995 collection to snakeskin with a buckle feature or patent black leather. Carolyn also wore a brown leather pair courtesy of Manolo Blahnik, notably in a shot of her leaving Bubby's with JFK Jr. in October 1997. In a 2024 *British Vogue* article centring around Carolyn's preferred footwear choices, Elise Taylor highlighted another element that may have come into play when selecting shoes for the day: "Having shoes that allowed her to navigate quickly through a human swarm of cameras was a safety choice just as much as a style one."

When the New York winters hit, Carolyn would whip out her trusted knee-high leather boots. She often wore them with her trademark midi skirts, and her collection is said to have developed over the years, including various labels but ultimately prioritizing Prada. Carolyn's rotation included a pair of black leather block heel boots and a cognac brown pair with a thin strap and buckle feature, famously worn as a part of her outfit when John introduced her to the press on their Tribeca doorstep in 1996.

OPPOSITE Carolyn and John at the Jacqueline Kennedy Onassis Medal Awards gala in New York City, 4 March 1997

ABOVE Carolyn and John walking to the subway in Tribeca, New York City, 10 October 1996

OPPOSITE Carolyn wearing her Prada snakeskin loafers alongside an Ann Demeulemeester coat in New York, circa 1996

ABOVE Carolyn goes for a pop of red with a Prada coat, worn during a morning walk with John and Friday in New York, 1997

THE COATS

Dressing for New York's chilly winters is no easy feat. But we all know who managed to do it while still looking like a million dollars. Carolyn's winter wardrobe has become another key aspect of her distinct, yet incredibly simple, fashion. Her coats in particular have become a specific interest for fans of her style.

Carolyn's Prada coats were among her preferred styles. She owned a camel-coloured model said to have been from the Autumn/Winter 1996 collection, seen in 1997 and 1998. At some point, the coat was gifted to RoseMarie Terenzio. It became such an iconic piece that it eventually sold at auction in March 2026 for a staggering US $192,000 or about £143,000. Carolyn also wore two other variations of the belted design, one in a black double-faced wool construction and another in a red mohair model with leather trim. In November 1996, Carolyn wore a green check Valentino coat from the Italian label's Autumn/Winter 1996 collection to attend a memorial service for the man who would have been her father-in-law, John F. Kennedy. This coat would also end up on sale through the Fashion Auction in 2026.

You'll also find Carolyn's leopard print coat on plenty of mood boards featuring her most adored looks. Reportedly sourced at a flea market in Paris, the double-breasted style was another one that RoseMarie Terenzio was gifted by her generous friend, Carolyn reportedly claiming, "It looks perfect on you. You should keep it. I've been photographed in it so many times [the media] are going to start making fun of me."

26

Bubby's
Bubby's
11
HUDS

“She was a very smart woman and she didn’t need to be told what to wear... She had a great eye.”

Narciso Rodriguez for WWD, *2024*

PREVIOUS PAGES Carolyn wearing her Prada camel coat in New York City, 15 March 1997

OPPOSITE The leopard print coat, seen here on a walk with John and Friday in December 1997, was sold at auction in 2024 for $33,600

ABOVE One of Carolyn's favourite Prada coat designs
on display at Sotheby's, 5 December 2024

ABOVE Carolyn in her trusty black Prada coat
(also shown opposite), 19 January 1997

THE BAGS

Carolyn's approach to bags is another area that could be closely analysed as a representation of her overall style philosophy. She had a small collection of styles that she wore repeatedly over the years. Each offered a minimalist design, premium quality and supreme versatility. Here, we'll examine the key styles she was spotted wearing throughout the nineties.

In a 2012 piece with the *New York Post*, RoseMarie spoke of CBK's relationship with her bags, stating, "Carolyn had handbags, but she didn't have 75 handbags. I don't think it existed back then, but I can't imagine Carolyn putting her name on a wait list for a bag." The Prada Spazzolato tote has become one of the bags most closely associated with Carolyn. She first began sporting the patent leather style in 1996 and continued to be seen with it over the following years. The style was distinctly nineties, and despite the designer label, the bag was made for everyday life. Carolyn was seen making full use of the bag as it overflowed with notebooks and fashion magazines while she bolted between appointments. In 2022, Prada re-released a version of the style and named it after Carolyn, cementing the connection between CBK and the sleek design.

OPPOSITE Carrying her Prada Spazzolato tote bag, Carolyn is spotted in a Chanel camellia-print dress and Manolo Blahnik slingbacks following the funeral of friend Billy Way, where it's rumoured the family requested guests to avoid black clothing, 16 July 1996

Another style spotted on Carolyn's arm was her beloved Birkin 40. It's important to note that though the Hermès design was far from a realistic option for the average woman in the 1990s, it wasn't quite the status symbol that it has become today, reserved for the ultra-rich. The Birkin 40 was originally designed as a holdall for Jane Birkin's travels, offering plenty of space for her essentials. Carolyn wore the bag religiously from 1996 until her death in 1999. Some of the most famous images of Carolyn with her Birkin 40 include a June day in 1997 when she held the bag under her arm while hailing a cab, wearing a simple black top, a pair of jeans and some flip-flops. She was also seen sporting it on plenty of occasions – walking through Tribeca with her husband, wearing corduroy trousers and a roll-neck or a white shirt and chinos. But perhaps one of the occasions which tells us most about Carolyn's approach to dressing and relationship with her Birkin 40 is captured by grainy images of Carolyn riding the subway with the bag, half open, placed on the floor.

OPPOSITE Carolyn returning home carrying the Prada Spazzolato tote, 9 March 1997

ABOVE Carolyn, carrying a leather envelope clutch, smiling with Lee Radziwill and Herbert Ross at the *George* magazine anniversary party in New York City, 5 November 1997

ABOVE Carolyn heads to Hyannis with her Hermès Birkin 40 in 1997

ABOVE Carolyn wears a Gucci headscarf, dark top, jeans
and Prada bag as she and John go shopping in Boston, 1996

THE JEANS

Carolyn's love for denim can be seen as a testament to the power that denim had over the fashion world in the nineties, while also reflecting her determination to present herself in a way that felt authentic. Denim's rich semiotic meaning meant that Carolyn was able to communicate herself, whether consciously or not, as a regular person, going about her business in New York City. Her choice of trousers probably increased her relatability and, in turn, her likeability to many. Fashion theorists have long studied the power of jeans. Daniel Miller, a UK anthropologist dedicated to studying blue jeans, explains: "Jeans convey the idea of being a simple, unaffected, everyday kind of person, friendly and inoffensive ... Jeans cause no bother, physically or socially."

Carolyn's preferred model of jeans is said to have been the Levi's 517s, a bootcut design first introduced in 1969. The model was designed as a men's jean and offered a slim leg which widened at the bottom to fit around the wearer's boots. The Levi's 517 has experienced a few changes over the years, adapting to shoppers' preferences, but the model remains available today. The former publicist would be seen wearing jeans – thought to be this style throughout the nineties – on strolls with her husband, at the Kennedys' Hyannisport compound or shopping in Manhattan.

Another style seen on Carolyn was a more carpenter-style jean. Baggier in fit, this model features a longer leg and notable back strap from the side seam to the back patch pocket. Some have claimed this to be a style from Gap, but the more likely answer is that these are Calvin Klein's from the brand's Autumn/Winter 1996 collection.

ABOVE Carolyn, John and dog
Friday at Teterboro Airport
on 12 October 1998

ABOVE On 11 June 1997, Carolyn stepped out wearing baggy carpenter jeans, a black top said to be from Gap, flip-flops and her Hermès Birkin 40 bag

THE SUNGLASSES

For many of her everyday looks, Carolyn and her sunglasses are basically inseparable. Although sunglasses were surely part of her wardrobe before her marriage to JFK Jr., they became more frequently worn as press interest in her intensified. Her sunglasses became one of her signature pieces, demonstrating her impeccable taste while retaining some protection from the often-incessant paparazzi camera flashes.

Carolyn preferred a slim style that balanced a timeless essence with a touch of nineties charm. A few models made appearances during Carolyn's outings, but one pair seemed to be preferred above the rest. The Aldo from Selima Optique is defined by its oval-shaped lenses and sleek design. In a 2023 interview, Selima Optique's founder Selima Salaun shared her experience with Carolyn: "She bought one color, but then I made others for her because she was so obsessed with the style ... She had such a specific look, she was very chic. She never asked for pink or red or blue. It was tortoises, khakis, and neutrals." Selima Optique has since gone on to design two additional versions of the sunglasses, the Carolyn and the CBK. Carolyn was also spotted on rare occasions wearing other models, including the Oakley E-Wire sunglasses, which she wore in 1997 while shopping on Madison Avenue.

OPPOSITE Celebrating the 1998 Fourth of July weekend in Hyannisport, Carolyn is spotted wearing her Aldo sunglasses, white tee and black jeans

OPPOSITE Carolyn taking
a taxi in New York City,
27 February 1997

N.Y.C.-TAXI
7L10
TAXI FARE

OPPOSITE Carolyn wears her Oakley E-Wire sunglasses on a day out shopping in July 1997

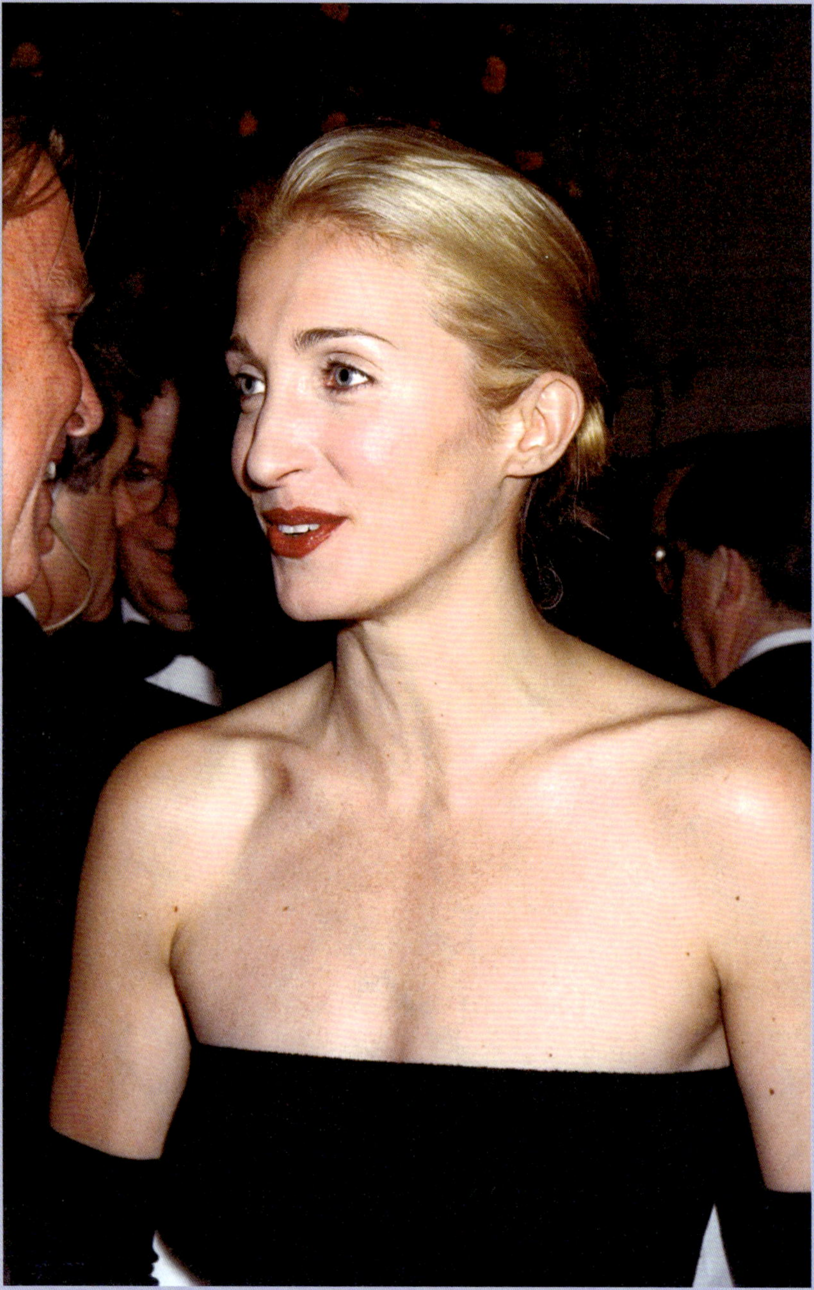

THE BEAUTY REGIME

Carolyn's approach to her hair and make-up appears to have followed a similar philosophy to her dressing – simple and not overthought. Though many speculate that her hair was often air-dried, we do know that she frequently made trips to her trusted salon to maintain the blonde colour that would end up being one of key aspects of her style. The exact date where she traded in her light brown strands for scattered platinum streaks isn't known, but her former colourist, Brad Johns, remarked that this took place sometime in 1995. Johns told *Newsweek* in October 1996, "She wanted to make it more interesting and beautiful ... Now it's a honey blond with big buttery chunks around the front." In November 1997, Maryellen Gordon, writing for *The New York Times,* knew who to credit for helping fashion move away from big volume towards something more understated: "Thanks to women like Julia Roberts and Carolyn Bessette-Kennedy, the hair look of the moment is straight and sleek." Kiehl's was said to be a favourite of both Carolyn and John, and Crème with Silk Groom, a moisturizing hair cream, was a staple in the couple's grooming kits. Her headbands were also a key part of her look throughout the 1990s, a tortoiseshell style being a firm favourite. The hair accessory was said to have been from the Charles Wahba brand, sourced from C.O. Bigelow, an apothecary that opened in New York's Greenwich Village in 1838.

OPPOSITE Carolyn showing her trademark simple make-up and hair at the Municipal Art Society Gala at Grand Central Terminal, 5 October 1998

Carolyn's make-up has also been a key point of interest over the years. It's been said that she wore products including the MAC Studio Fix Powder and Bobbi Brown eyeshadow in the shade "Bone", a light beige colour that ensured her look was kept natural. For evening events, Carolyn often wore a bright lip for a touch of glam. Among her go-to shades were Cranberry Veil from FACE Stockholm, a Swedish cosmetic brand with a shop in New York's SoHo, which Carolyn was said to frequent. The co-founder of FACE Stockholm said in an April 2026 article, "Cranberry really is a very special shade. It is a warm red, but not too bold and not too sheer. What made it so right for Carolyn, I think, is that it matched her effortless style." She is also said to have worn another Bobbi Brown product, this time a lipstick in the shade Ruby Stain.

Another aspect of Carolyn's approach to beauty was her preferred fragrances. In a 2016 interview with the *Daily Telegraph*, actor Liv Tyler, who once lived in the same building as Carolyn, recalled noticing her fragrance when the two hugged as they passed in the hall. Asking about it, she was told it was "a musk oil from a street vendor in New York. So I stopped at every table in the East and West Village and started collecting them." Abdul Kareem Egyptian Musk Oil was named in Carole Radziwill's memoir, *What Remains*, as Carolyn's signature scent. It's been said that Kiehl's Cucumber Essence Oil was another of her favourites.

OPPOSITE Sporting a red lip and an outfit courtesy of Yohji Yamamoto's Fall 1997 collection, Carolyn attends Giuseppe Verdi's *Macbeth* in Milan with John on 7 December 1997

"She never wore that much make-up – a sheer moisturizer foundation and probably a little eyeliner and mascara and her favorite Bobbi Brown Ruby Stain lip color."

RoseMarie Terenzio writes in
JFK Jr.: An Intimate Oral Biography

OPPOSITE Carolyn and John at the New York Municipal Art Society Gala on 1 March 1997

THE KNITWEAR

From Ralph Lauren turtlenecks to the Prada knit she wore in that famous "meet the press" look outside her and John's Tribeca loft after their wedding, Carolyn's affinity for knitwear is well documented. Certainly, the New York resident knew the power of a good jumper when it came to surviving the colder temperatures that the city is known to serve up in the winter months. While at Calvin Klein, Carolyn reportedly wore slip dresses and fisherman sweaters, inspiring colleagues with her ability to seamlessly flaunt contrasting textures. Wayne Scot Lukas, a former colleague of Carolyn's at Calvin Klein, shared on his social media, "Carolyn had a way of just throwing on a slip dress and adding a big, bulky sweater, and that became the look."

"Sometimes she would be wearing a fisherman's sweater, track pants, and sneakers, her hair wild," a former supervisor told Elizabeth Beller for her book on Carolyn, *Once Upon a Time*. Knits from TSE Cashmere, Calvin Klein and Jil Sander were also commonplace in her everyday outfits. Plenty of snaps of Carolyn at her most laidback also depict her in comfy knits – at small gatherings with friends and family or going about her daily life with her husband and dog.

OPPOSITE Carolyn and John in New York City, 15 November 1997

THE SKIRTS

Carolyn's love for skirts with hemlines that sat just below the knee meant that they quickly became one of the garments most associated with the former PR exec – even *Vogue* mentioned her directly when doing a story on the style in a 1999 issue ("Carolyn Bessette-Kennedy is the latest fan"). The camel Prada skirt worn to pose for the press in the summer of 1996 played a big role in CBK associating herself with the pencil skirt. This was undeniably one of her most well-known pieces, selling for US $30,000 at auction via The Fashion Auctioneer in early 2026.

Carolyn also owned skirts from Ann Demeulemeester, one of her favourite designers, according to RoseMarie Terenzio. One fan favourite was a leather style from the Belgian designer's Spring/Summer 1997 collection. Another favourite was a brown suede midi from Prada, worn alongside a black long-sleeve tee and slip-on flats from Manolo Blahnik during an outing in June 1998. Slip skirts, or bias-cut skirts, were also a mainstay in her wardrobe, sometimes making an appearance as a part of red-carpet looks, notably when Carolyn attended *The Warhol Look: Glamour, Style, Fashion* exhibition gala, hosted by the Whitney Museum in November 1997. Carolyn stuck to her trusted Yohji Yamamoto for both the floor-grazing skirt and off-the-shoulder top. She wore a similar rendition of this outfit, though this time opting for a classic black pencil skirt, nearly two years later while attending a Ralph Lauren dinner in Mayfair on 4 May 1999 with JFK Jr.

OPPOSITE Carolyn wearing a dark top, Prada skirt and Manolo Blahnik slip-on flats while out in New York, 1998

HÆR

I

CHAPTER 4

EGACY

INTRODUCTION

Following the plane crash that claimed the life of Carolyn, JFK Jr. and her sister, Lauren, many of the major news outlets carried statements from the fashion elite, sharing their memories of Carolyn. Oscar de la Renta told *WWD* that he saw Carolyn as "the incarnation of modern style". Donatella Versace told *New York Magazine*, "Any entrance Carolyn made, she made a statement. Apart from the clothes she wore, she had a way of moving her head and smiling, and her eyes were so expressive, she would always seem to be looking right at you." One piece dedicated to CBK after her death mentioned reports alleging that she had purchased a black Yves Saint Laurent dress from Saks Fifth Avenue the day of the fateful flight, reportedly planning to wear it to Rory Kennedy's wedding the next day. Alber Elbaz, the creative director of YSL at the time, reportedly took inspiration from Carolyn when designing, according to a 1999 article in the *New York Post*. A few months later, Chloë Sevigny wore the same design on the red carpet.

OPPOSITE The cover of the August 1999 issue of *Vanity Fair*, paying homage to Carolyn and John following their deaths a few weeks earlier

VANITY FAIR
September 1999/$3.95
CAROLYN BESSETTE KENNEDY
A 10-PAGE PORTFOLIO BY BRUCE WEBER
JOHN F. KENNEDY JR.
A REMEMBRANCE BY DAVID MICHAELIS
DOMINICK DUNNE ON THE DU PONT MURDER
PATRICIA BOSWORTH ON ELIA KAZAN
BRYAN BURROUGH ON THE GHOST OF EVEREST
BRUCE HANDY ON PEE-WEE HERMAN
KIM MASTERS ON BOB DALY AND TERRY SEMEL
DAVID MARANISS ON VINCE LOMBARDI

"She was one of the most iconic, beautiful and stylish women of our time, who epitomised elegant, easy and flawless chic."

Jayne Pickering, former
Marie Claire *Fashion Director*

OPPOSITE Carolyn smiling at a benefit dinner in New York City, autumn 1998

HIGHLIGH
Fashion

HER INFLUENCE ON THE FASHION WORLD

In the years since her passing, plenty of designers and brands have openly spoken about their work being influenced by Carolyn's style. Carolina Herrera's Spring/Summer 2024 collection notes credit Carolyn, stating the aim of the collection was to evoke "the casual glamour and ease of the eternal American muse, Carolyn Bessette-Kennedy". Many also speculate that labels like Celine, Khaite, The Row and Toteme have also looked to Carolyn's nineties outfits for inspiration over the years, all demonstrating an austere approach that CBK executed perfectly. In 2024, Sporty & Rich released campaign imagery that people were quick to point out resembled much of the famous "walking shots" of Carolyn and JFK Jr. around New York. In 2026, Reformation released a collection that featured an array of outfits nearly identical to some of CBK's greatest hits (covered in previous chapters), even going as far as offering an ivory silk dress with a cowl neckline reminiscent of the style worn by Carolyn on her big day in 1996.

PREVIOUS PAGES Pieces said to have belonged to CBK appeared as a part of the 2024 "Fashion Icons" exhibition at Sotheby's, New York

“The obsession now is legit. She was legit... She really was effortlessly stylish and beautiful.”

Guinevere Van Seenus for Harper’s Bazaar, *2026*

Beyond inspiring designers and brands directly, Carolyn's influence on some of the most well-known names in the press has also been successfully documented. Some stars who are most known for their CBK-inspired looks include Bella Hadid, Hailey Bieber and Kendall Jenner, with the latter reportedly referencing Carolyn's blonde hair to her colourist Jenna Perry in 2024. Perry told *Vogue*, "She is really inspired by the nineties and Carolyn Bessette-Kennedy right now." Meghan Markle is also known to be a fan of CBK's style, notably referencing her wedding dress when asked about her favourite bridal gown in a 2016 interview with *Glamour*.

OPPOSITE Alaïa's Autumn/Winter 2026 collection was one of the many which the press compared to CBK's nineties looks

THE NEXT GENERATION

Although Carolyn's fashion has been a source of inspiration for many insiders and lovers of minimalist dressing over the years, the rise of "quiet luxury" around 2023 meant that she was cropping up on mood boards of a new generation. In the summer of 2025, it was announced that American TV producer Ryan Murphy was working on a miniseries with FX/Disney+, which would look at the relationship between Carolyn Bessette and JFK Jr. Quickly, the fashion world went into a frenzy, speculating about how Carolyn's beloved looks would translate on screen. Murphy himself later acknowledged CBK's status as a kind of "religious figure in style circles", following the backlash sparked by the programme's promotional images. The criticism ultimately led him to replace the previous, unnamed costume designer with Rudy Mance, who was brought in specifically to recreate Carolyn's looks more faithfully. Mance has spoken about the lengths he and his team went to ensure Carolyn's outfits accurately reflected what she would have worn, studying images of the former publicist and borrowing from collectors, scouring shops and second-hand platforms like Etsy and eBay for

OPPOSITE A January 2026 *Vogue* piece stated, "the model's latest look proves she's probably got some CBK saved on her own Pinterest board", referencing this look from Bella Hadid

the perfect pieces. Mance even managed to find the exact fabric used to create her legendary wedding dress. "It's one of the most iconic dresses to have ever been created and photographed. So, I wanted to pay my respects to her, but also to Narciso," he told *Vogue* in a story from March 2026.

Murphy's series created significant interest in CBK from younger generations, and quickly, snaps of the nineties icon were appearing across social media at a volume not witnessed before. The blonde "style stoic" (as *Elle* UK's Naomi May dubbed her in a 2024 article) was no longer a muse reserved for Gen X and millennials with an affinity for understated looks – now she was being referenced by top fashion influencers across TikTok and Instagram, with countless accounts offering tips on how to recreate Carolyn's trademark style.

OPPOSITE Some of Carolyn's favourite pieces were also spotted as a part of one of Stephanie Broek's outfits for Paris Fashion Week in March 2026

One piece dug into the impact of Carolyn's 2026 social media boom following the release of *Love Story*, with *Glamour*'s Grace McCarty sharing that the heightened interest led to increased sales for plenty of brands linked to the former PR exec. There was an uplift of 2,700 per cent in online sales for CBK's Aldo sunglasses model from Selima Optique, and Bobbi Brown's team revealed: "Notably, on-site searches for Crushed Lipstick in Ruby have increased 600 per cent year on year over the past month, with retailer sales increasing by as much as 286 per cent year on year – a trend that has continued as new episodes have aired." Though we don't know the demographics of these sales, it's safe to say that the phenomenon of CBK is far from forgotten.

OPPOSITE CBK's influence could be spotted across various outfits at Paris Fashion Week in March 2026, including this minimalist look worn by Isabelle Hartmann

“She was minimalism with character – she wasn’t sterile or boring.”

Wes Gordon, Creative Director of Carolina Herrera

OPPOSITE A model walks the runway of the Carolina Herrera ready-to-wear Spring/Summer 2024 fashion show, 12 September 2023, New York City

CONCLUSION

Over the years, many have weighed in on why they believe Carolyn's style continues to resonate with people around the world, even decades after her death. Sotheby's Fashion Specialist, Lucy Bishop, credits this to Carolyn's understanding of "the power that fashion can hold in the everyday life of a woman." Others, like Julia Rabinowitsch, founder of The Millennial Decorator, told *Vogue* in 2024 that Carolyn's popularity may be a product of shifting priorities in how many women dress now: "There's so much interest in this vintage, timeless way of dressing ... Carolyn was a perfect embodiment of that." The topic of sustainability is worth examining in relation to CBK's enduring influence. Bethan Holt of the *Daily Telegraph* spoke about this to *Marie Claire* in 2019. "With the conversation around sustainability and timelessness, and investing in [forever] pieces, her look is never going to date," Holt said. Elizabeth Beller, author of *Once Upon a Time*, reportedly shares this viewpoint, telling Vanessa Friedman of *The New York Times* in 2023 that she believes part of Carolyn's popularity after all these years is because she "resonates with the cultural vibe of 'stealth wealth' and interest in sustainability."

OPPOSITE Carolyn at the Krizia fashion retrospective at the Grey Art Gallery in April 1999

But we know that style goes beyond the clothes we slip into each day. Much of its power lies in the way in which they're worn. This is something Carolyn proved throughout her years in the public eye. Journalist Naomi May summarized this in her 2024 piece for *Elle* UK: "You can't know or teach that which Bessette-Kennedy inherently imbibed, but you can take lessons from her innate comfort with herself." And perhaps it was that comfort in herself that enabled her to confidently select the pieces which worked best for her rather than succumbing to pressure to follow each and every trend of the time. Of course, she didn't ignore them entirely, but from most accounts, her relationship to clothes was careful and considered – quite the contrast to the often-vapid consumption habits that have become normalized today.

OPPOSITE Big smiles from Carolyn at the May 1999 "Newman's Own" *George* Awards

In a 2016 article with *Town & Country* magazine, Patricia Mears, deputy director at the Fashion Institute of Technology, relayed her thoughts on the difference between Carolyn's style ethos and the prevalent approach today: "I don't think there is anybody like that anymore. Everything is about social media and how you can attract attention [now]. That was the opposite of what she wanted to do." In reality, Carolyn's style appeal has likely withstood the test of time for several reasons, though some commentators initially assumed it would not. Eleanor Lambert, founder of the International Best Dressed Hall of Fame List on which Carolyn often appeared, told *Harpers & Queen* in 1999: "She wasn't in the public eye long enough to influence fashion long term ... But she was very much admired by the fashion editors and the press." What's clear is that Carolyn has exceeded such expectations and stands now as one of the most influential dressers in modern history.

OPPOSITE Carolyn and Friday enjoy a brisk winter's day in January 1998

PX·430K

CREDITS

The publishers would like to thank the following sources for their kind permission to reproduce the pictures in this book.

Alamy:
AP Photo/Charles Krupa 97, John Barrett/Globe Photos/ZUMAPRESS.com 20-21, Laura Cavanaugh/Globe Photos/ZUMAPRESS.com 125, 126, Globe Photos/ZUMAPRESS.com 147, LaPresse 168-169, 174, 207, Patti McConville 93, Henry McGee/MediaPunch 165, Sipa US 101, UPI/Alamy Live News: 188-189

Diggzy / BACKGRID 194

Bobby Dimarzo/POLARIS 23

Getty
185, Evan Agostini 135, 148, Bettmann Archive 52, Peter Bischoff 110, Brooks Kraft LLC/Sygma 71, John Calabrese/Penske Media 70, RJ Capak/WireImage 72, 82, Stephane Cardinale/Sygma 90-91, George Chinsee/WWD/Penske Media 40, Richard Corkery/NY Daily News Archive 60-61, 66, 78, 172, Jean-Claude Deutsch/Paris Match 96, Steve Eichner/Penske Media142, 160, Kyle Ericksen 45, Fairchild Archive/Penske Media 34-35, Steven Ferdman 154, Diane Freed 204, Ron Galella, Ltd./Ron Galella Collection 48, 144, 83, 102, Giovanni Giannoni/Penske Media 69, 75, 79, 106, 107, 121, Trevor Gillespie186, Thomas Iannaccone/Penske Media 27, Justin Ide/Newsmakers 114, Chris Kleponis/AFP 76, Wendy Maeda/The Boston Globe 24, Arnaldo Magnani / Liaison Agency 54-55, Tyler Mallory 113, Patrick McMullan36-37, 38-39, 42, 46, 50-51, Joyce Naltchayan/AFP 88, Jon Naso/NY Daily News Archive 62, Robin Platzer 177, Donato Sardella/Penske Media 68, 109, Moritz Scholz 197, 198, Lawrence Schwartzwald/Sygma 59, 116, 119, 122, 136, 141, 150-151, 155, 157, 159, 170-171, 178, Jim Steinfeldt/Michael Ochs Archives 28-29, Monique Stienstra 203, Allan Tannenbaum 146, Bill Turnbull/NY Daily News Archive 164, David Turner/Penske Media 8-9, 30, Victor Virgile/Gamma-Rapho 201, Tom Wargacki/WireImage 56, Eric Weiss/Penske Media 33, WWD 193

Dawn Klavon 17

Shutterstock
11, Matt Baron/BEI 12, Boston Herald 84-85, 162, DMI/The LIFE Picture Collection 81, Globe Photos/ZUMA Press Wire 19, 128, 139, 152-153, Alex Oliveira 105, 180, Sipa 6-7, 129, Charles Sykes 98, Kevin Wisniewski 65, 74, 130, 161, 167

Denis Reggie 94